# Instant Wijmo Widgets How-to

Learn how to use Wijmo tools to speed up UI development and browser compatibility through practical recipes

**Tochi Eke-Okoro**

BIRMINGHAM - MUMBAI

# Instant Wijmo Widgets How-to

First published: March 2013

Production Reference: 1200313

Published by Packt Publishing Ltd.
Livery Place
35 Livery Street
Birmingham B3 2PB, UK.

ISBN 978-1-78216-186-8

www.packtpub.com

# Credits

**Author**
Tochi Eke-Okoro

**Reviewer**
Joe Zimmerman

**Acquisition Editor**
Kartikey Pandey

**Commissioning Editor**
Ameya Sawant

**Technical Editor**
Kirti Pujari

**Copy Editor**
Aditya Nair

**Project Coordinator**
Esha Thakker

**Proofreader**
Lauren Tobon

**Production Coordinator**
Nilesh R. Mohite

**Cover Work**
Nilesh R. Mohite

**Cover Image**
Sheetal Aute

# About the Author

**Tochi Eke-Okoro** is currently the Tech Lead of Front End Engineering at Joor Inc. He has worked with billion-dollar companies and startups as both a backend and frontend developer. He enjoys fiddling with Object Oriented JavaScript, hacking jQuery plugins, Ajax, JSON, PHP scripting, Terminal, and C++. He also enjoys playing mission-based video and sport games, chess, and manga animations. He lives in Newark, New Jersey, with his beautiful wife and son.

I wish to dedicate this book to my loving wife, Obioma, for her ceaseless support and encouragement through the writing of this book. My regards to my wonderful parents, who brought me up the right way, and to my family and friends.

# About the Reviewer

**Joe Zimmerman** is a 25-year-old web developer who specializes in the frontend and is nearly obsessed with JavaScript, which he regularly blogs about on `http://www.joezimjs.com`. He has also written for *Adobe Developer Connection* (`http://www.adobe.com/devnet.html`), *Smashing Magazine* (`http://www.smashingmagazine.com`), and *Nettuts+* (`http://net.tutsplus.com`). Some of his articles have also been featured in magazines such as *Hacker Monthly* and *Appliness*.

He currently works as a web developer for Kaplan University's School of Professional and Continuing Education. As of right now, his core responsibility is maintaining the Schweser website.

> I'm a devoted Christian and God has blessed me with a wife and two wonderful little boys (so far). I'd like to say thanks to those guys for having patience with me while I'm working on my blog and reviewing books.

# www.PacktPub.com

## Support files, eBooks, discount offers and more

You might want to visit www.PacktPub.com for support files and downloads related to your book.

Did you know that Packt offers eBook versions of every book published, with PDF and ePub files available? You can upgrade to the eBook version at www.PacktPub.com and as a print book customer, you are entitled to a discount on the eBook copy. Get in touch with us at service@packtpub.com for more details.

At www.PacktPub.com, you can also read a collection of free technical articles, sign up for a range of free newsletters and receive exclusive discounts and offers on Packt books and eBooks.

http://PacktLib.PacktPub.com

Do you need instant solutions to your IT questions? PacktLib is Packt's online digital book library. Here, you can access, read and search across Packt's entire library of books.

## Why Subscribe?

- ▶ Fully searchable across every book published by Packt
- ▶ Copy and paste, print and bookmark content
- ▶ On demand and accessible via web browser

## Free Access for Packt account holders

If you have an account with Packt at www.PacktPub.com, you can use this to access PacktLib today and view nine entirely free books. Simply use your login credentials for immediate access.

I wish to dedicate this book to my loving wife Obioma for her ceaseless support and encouragement through the writing of this book.

# Table of Contents

# Preface

This book opens the reader to a world of aesthetic user interface widgets made available by Wijmo. It exhibits, via a step-wise approach, simple methods of creating and customizing various widgets, and how to display them. This will serve as an invaluable asset to a curious web developer seeking aesthetic features to deploy, a UI developer looking for cool widgets to hasten things up, or a student who needs a live calendar of events to attend.

## What this book covers

*Bar chart (Simple)* illustrates how to create and customize a Wijmo bar chart widget.

*Column bar chart (Simple)* explains how to convert a regular Wijmo bar chart to a column bar chart widget.

*Stacked bar chart (Simple)* shows how to create and customize a stacked bar chart widget.

*Animation and live data (Intermediate)* illustrates how to stream live data and also have an animated presentation.

*Bubble chart (Intermediate)* shows how to create and customize a bubble chart widget.

*Calendar (Intermediate)* illustrates how to create and customize a calendar widget.

*Grids (Advanced)* explains how to create and customize a grid widget. It also shows how to make the grid have editable fields on the fly.

*Data source (Advanced)* shows how to retrieve and display data from a given data source.

*Using Wijmo with KnockoutJS (Advanced)* illustrates how to integrate Knockout JS in Wijmo to facilitate widget functionality. This is very useful in binding events to a grid widget.

*ThemeRoller (Advanced)* explains via a step-wise process, how to create and customize themes.

# What you need for this book

You will need some knowledge of HTML, CSS, native JavaScript, and jQuery.

It is also necessary to know how to use any code editor and how to run code files on a browser.

# Who this book is for

This book is for web developers, user interface (UI) enthusiasts, and anyone interested in getting fully acquainted with the Wijmo library and widgets.

The book will be an invaluable asset to anyone who is in need of UI widgets to beautify or create aesthetic features on their web application.

# Conventions

In this book, you will find a number of styles of text that distinguish between different kinds of information. Here are some examples of these styles, and an explanation of their meaning.

Code words in text are shown as follows: "We can include other contexts through the use of the `include` directive."

A block of code is set as follows:

```
$("table").wijgrid({
    columns: columns,
    data: content,
    allowEditing: true
});
```

When we wish to draw your attention to a particular part of a code block, the relevant lines or items are set in bold:

```
$("table").wijgrid({
    columns: columns,
    data: content,
  allowEditing: true

});
```

**New terms** and **important words** are shown in bold. Words that you see on the screen, in menus or dialog boxes for example, appear in the text like this: "clicking the **Next** button moves you to the next screen".

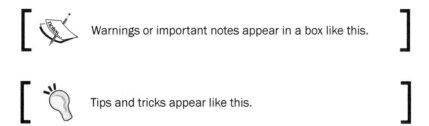

> Warnings or important notes appear in a box like this.

> Tips and tricks appear like this.

# Reader feedback

Feedback from our readers is always welcome. Let us know what you think about this book—what you liked or may have disliked. Reader feedback is important for us to develop titles that you really get the most out of.

To send us general feedback, simply send an e-mail to feedback@packtpub.com, and mention the book title via the subject of your message.

If there is a topic that you have expertise in and you are interested in either writing or contributing to a book, see our author guide on www.packtpub.com/authors.

# Customer support

Now that you are the proud owner of a Packt book, we have a number of things to help you to get the most from your purchase.

## Errata

Although we have taken every care to ensure the accuracy of our content, mistakes do happen. If you find a mistake in one of our books—maybe a mistake in the text or the code—we would be grateful if you would report this to us. By doing so, you can save other readers from frustration and help us improve subsequent versions of this book. If you find any errata, please report them by visiting http://www.packtpub.com/support, selecting your book, clicking on the **errata submission form** link, and entering the details of your errata. Once your errata are verified, your submission will be accepted and the errata will be uploaded on our website, or added to any list of existing errata, under the Errata section of that title. Any existing errata can be viewed by selecting your title from http://www.packtpub.com/support.

# Piracy

Piracy of copyright material on the Internet is an ongoing problem across all media. At Packt, we take the protection of our copyright and licenses very seriously. If you come across any illegal copies of our works, in any form, on the Internet, please provide us with the location address or website name immediately so that we can pursue a remedy.

Please contact us at copyright@packtpub.com with a link to the suspected pirated material.

We appreciate your help in protecting our authors, and our ability to bring you valuable content.

# Questions

You can contact us at questions@packtpub.com if you are having a problem with any aspect of the book, and we will do our best to address it.

# Instant Wijmo Widgets How-to

There has always been the need to quickly create user interface widgets that specialize in providing a specific service for a user or a group of users. The team at Wijmo has made a library of such widgets readily available for customized usage. This book focuses on introducing most of the common widgets and how they are used. *Instant Wijmo Widgets How-to* approaches tasks via a step-wise process that makes the reader's learning and practice experience worthwhile.

## Bar chart (Simple)

According to Wikipedia, a *bar chart* or *bar graph* is a chart with rectangular bars with lengths proportional to the values that they represent. The bars can be plotted vertically or horizontally. A vertical bar chart is sometimes called a column bar chart.

## Getting ready

Before we fully jump into bar charts, it is important to have some insight into Wijmo dependencies and how to reference them in our source code.

| Wijmo Dependency | Download URL |
| --- | --- |
| Wijmo Complete CDN (87 KB) | `http://cdn.wijmo.com/jquery.wijmo-complete.all.2.0.0.min.js` |
| Wijmo Open CDN (52 KB) | `http://cdn.wijmo.com/jquery.wijmo-open.all.2.0.0.min.js` |
| jQuery 1.7.1 (minified) | `http://ajax.aspnetcdn.com/ajax/jquery/jquery-1.7.1.min.js` |
| jQuery UI (minified) | `http://ajax.aspnetcdn.com/ajax/jquery.ui/1.8.17/jquery-ui.min.js` |
| Wijmo complete CSS | `http://cdn.wijmo.com/jquery.wijmo-complete.all.2.0.0.min.css` |
| Wijmo theme CSS | `http://cdn.wijmo.com/themes/rocket/jquery-wijmo.css` |

Having listed the requisite Wijmo dependencies, we will see how to reference them in any project and customize them further. All the latest dependencies can be found at `http://wijmo.com/downloads/#wijmo-cdn`.

## How to do it...

1. Create an HTML file and reference the dependencies listed in the preceding table. We can achieve this by inserting the links listed in the preceding table.

```html
<html>
    <head>
    <!--jQuery References-->
    <script src="http://ajax.aspnetcdn.com/ajax/jquery/jquery-1.7.1.min.js"
        type="text/javascript"></script>
    <script src="http://ajax.aspnetcdn.com/ajax/jquery.ui/1.8.17/jquery-ui.min.js"
        type="text/javascript"></script>
    <!--Wijmo Widgets JavaScript-->
    <script src="http://cdn.wijmo.com/jquery.wijmo-open.all.2.0.0.min.js"
        type="text/javascript"></script>
    <script src=http://cdn.wijmo.com/jquery.wijmo-complete.all.2.0.0.min.js"
        type="text/javascript"></script>
```

```
<!--Theme-->
<link href="http://cdn.wijmo.com/themes/rocket/jquery-wijmo.css"
rel="stylesheet"
        type="text/css" title="rocket-jqueryui" />
<!--Wijmo Widgets CSS-->
<link href="http://cdn.wijmo.com/jquery.wijmo-complete.
all.2.0.0.min.css"
 rel="stylesheet" type="text/css" />
    </head>
    <body></body>
</html>
```

2. The `wijbarchart` object needs a target in the HTML document to render itself to. Create a `div` tag within the HTML tags, with a reference ID or class for `wijbarchart` to render to.

```
<div id="wijbarchart" class="ui-widget ui-widget-content ui-
corner-all" style="width:    400px;height: 300px"></div>
```

3. Let us initialize the `wijbarchart` object and populate it with some data. This can be achieved via the following jQuery code:

```
<script id="scriptInit" type="text/javascript">
  //wait for the page to completely load...
        $(document).ready(function () {
            $("#wijbarchart").wijbarchart({

        //define the values for x and y axes...
                axis: {
                 y: {
                      text: "Total Automobile Sales (Per Hundred
Thousand)"
                   },
                   x: {
                       text: ""
                   }
                 },
        //the hint will display on hover of the chart
                hint: {
                    content: function () {
                        return this.data.label + '\n ' + this.y +
' ';
                    }
                 },
        //The chart's title or header
                header: {
                    text: "US Toyota Automobile Statistics (Dummy
Data)"
                 },
```

```
            //seriesList defines the label, legend and data for x and y...
                seriesList: [{
                    label: "US",
                    legendEntry: true,
                    data: { x: ['Toyota Camry', 'Toyota Corolla',
'Toyota Sienna'],
        y:    [12.35, 21.50, 30.56] }
                }],
            //define the color, stroke and opacity for the chart
                seriesStyles: [{
                    fill: "#8ede43", stroke: "#7fc73c", opacity:
0.8
                }],

                seriesHoverStyles: [{
"stroke-width": "1.5", opacity: 1
                }]
            });
        });
    </script>
```

4.  Now we save the code and run the widget by launching the HTML file in any web
    browser of our choice. The `wijbarchart` object shown will be similar to the
    following screenshot:

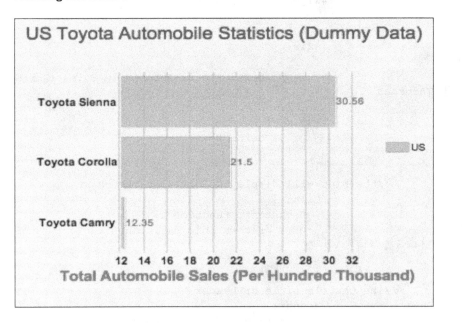

## There's more...

There are various aspects of the `wijbarchart` object one might want to customize. Let us customize the appearance of the `wijbarchart` object by changing the color of the bars, applying some gradient to it, and specifying the opacity.

### Changing the appearance of our wijbarchart object

Changing the appearance of a Wijmo bar chart is easily achievable by updating the `seriesStyles` property as follows:

```
seriesStyles: [{
            fill: "40-#BD0070-#718680", stroke: "#1261C0",
    opacity: 0.5
            }]
```

The `fill` property of the object in the `seriesStyles` array is set to the gradient value `"40-#BD0070-#718680"`. If we run the code after replacing the previous `seriesStyles` value with the new one, we will have something like this:

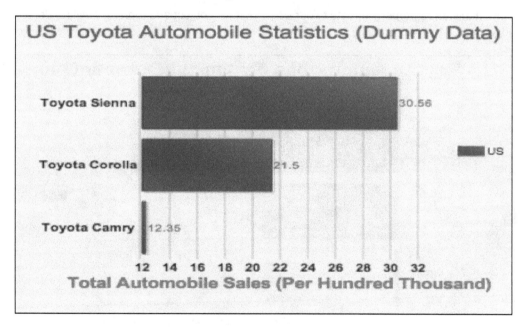

Another useful customization is the ability to rotate labels on the axes. This will slant the labels in a specified angle of your choice. To achieve this, we would have to update the `axis` property of our `wijbarchart` object as follows:

```
axis: {
        y: {
              text: "Total Automobile Sales",

        },
        x: {
              text: "",
              labels: {
                    style: {
                          rotation: -45
                    }
              }
        }
    },
```

Applying this `axis` property update to our `wijbarchart` object and running it will render a widget similar to this:

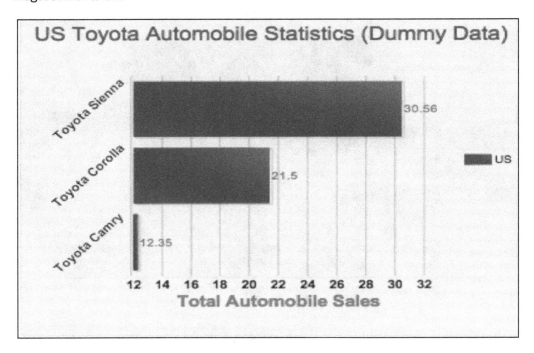

This completes our section on creating a simple Wijmo bar chart widget. This has obviously been a simple and painless process. We set up all references or links to the requisite Wijmo files, which are available and hosted in the Wijmo CDN, as listed in the preceding table. We continued to develop the `wijbarchart` object by setting the various configurations required for a proper widget display, such as the `axis`, `hint`, `header`, `seriesList`, `seriesStyles`, and `seriesHoverStyles` properties.

These configurations, also known as options, are not the only ones available for creating a bar chart widget. The team at Wijmo actually did create a ton of options for user customizations; a few useful Wijmo bar chart options are listed as follows:

- `animation`: This option handles all animation effects, such as easing and duration. All charts are animated by default. By animation, I refer to the duration for completely drawing the chart. Its default value is `{enabled: true, duration: 400}`.

  Here is an example of how to use the `animation` property:

  ```
  $("#wijbarchart").wijbarchart({
  animation:{
      enabled:true,
      duration:800
     }...
  });
  ```

- `footer`: This option designates the footer of the chart widget. Its default value is `{visible:false, style:{fill:"#fff", stroke:"none"}, textStyle:{fill:"#000", stroke:"none"}, compass:"south", orientation:"horizontal"}`.

  Here is an example of how to use the `footer` property:

  ```
  $("#wijbarchart").wijbarchart({
      footer: {
          text:"widget footer",
          style:{
              fill:"#f1f1f1",
              stroke:"#010101"
          }
      }
  });
  ```

- `horizontal`: This option value determines whether to render a horizontal or vertical bar chart. Its default value is `true`.

  Here is an example of how to use the `horizontal` property:

  ```
  $("#wijbarchart").wijbarchart({
      horizontal: true
     });
  ```

For more information on Wijmo bar chart options, please visit the Wijmo bar chart wiki at `http://wijmo.com/wiki/index.php/Barchart`.

# Column bar chart (Simple)

A column bar chart widget is slightly different from the regular bar chart widget we previously created. Remember we also had a look at some of the useful and common options used by most Wijmo developers. The last one we listed was the `horizontal` option of type Boolean. The default value of the `horizontal` option is `true`. This implies that the bar chart will be rendered in a horizontal layout by default.

## Getting ready

For the creation of our first column bar chart, we shall proceed by setting the `horizontal` option to `false`, using the same code used for the previous bar chart we had created. Here's our new complete code:

```html
<html>
    <head>
<!--jQuery References-->
<script src="http://ajax.aspnetcdn.com/ajax/jquery/jquery-1.7.1.min.
js" type="text/javascript"></script>
<script src="http://ajax.aspnetcdn.com/ajax/jquery.ui/1.8.17/jquery-
ui.min.js" type="text/javascript"></script>
<!--Wijmo Widgets JavaScript-->
<script src="http://cdn.wijmo.com/jquery.wijmo-open.all.2.0.0.min.js"
type="text/javascript"></script>
<script src="http://cdn.wijmo.com/jquery.wijmo-complete.all.2.0.0.min.
js" type="text/javascript"></script>
<!--Theme-->
<link href="http://cdn.wijmo.com/themes/rocket/jquery-wijmo.css"
rel="stylesheet" type="text/css" title="rocket-jqueryui" />
<!--Wijmo Widgets CSS-->
<link href="http://cdn.wijmo.com/jquery.wijmo-complete.all.2.0.0.min.
css" rel="stylesheet" type="text/css" />
</head>
<body>
<div id="wijbarchart" class="ui-widget ui-widget-content ui-corner-
all" style="width: 400px;
height: 300px">
</div>

<script id="scriptInit" type="text/javascript">
        $(document).ready(function () {
```

```
//activating the wijbarchart function on #wijbarchart
        $("#wijbarchart").wijbarchart({
        horizontal: false,//makes it vertical
        axis: { //set up the x and y axes
            y: {
                text: "Total Automation Sales",

            },
            x: {
                text: "",
                labels: {
                    style: {
                        rotation: -45
                    }
                }
            }
        },

            hint: { //hint text when hovering over chart
                content: function () {
                    return this.data.label + '\n ' + this.y + '';
                }
            },

            header: {//chart title
                text: "US Toyota Automobile Statistics (Dummy
Data)"
            },
    //data for chart representing each column
            seriesList: [{
                label: "US",
                legendEntry: true,
                data: { x: ['Toyota Camry', 'Toyota Corolla',
'Toyota Sienna'], y: [12.35, 21.50, 30.56] }
            }],

            seriesStyles: [{
                fill: "40-#BD0070-#718680", stroke: "#1261C0",
opacity: 0.7
            }],

            seriesHoverStyles: [{ "stroke-width": "1.5", opacity:
1
            }]
        });
    });
    </script>
    </body>
</html>
```

Notice from the preceding code, which we will hereon refer to as the **main code**, that we set the `horizontal` option to `false`. Now, when we run the main code, we should see a column bar chart widget as follows:

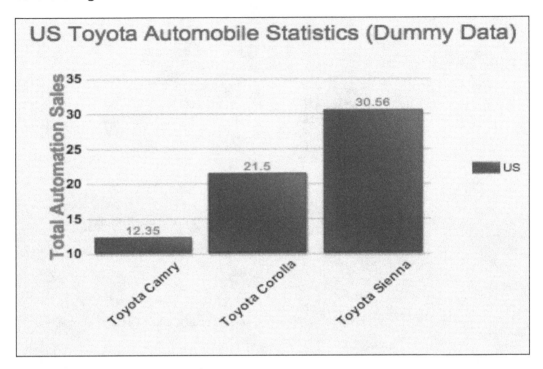

That's how simple switching from a regular bar chart to a column bar chart is. The choice between either of the two bar charts is usually dependent on user preference.

## How to do it...

We reference the Wijmo dependencies as follows:

1. After the page loads, we set the `horizontal` property to `false`.

2. The `x` and `y` properties are set, and `y` is rotated at `-45` degrees, which rotates the labels for Toyota Camry, Toyota Corolla, and Toyota Sienna.

3. We set the `hint` property, which is displayed on hovering over the chart.

4. We set the `header` property, which is displayed atop the grid.

5. For the `seriesList` property, we have a `data` subproperty that holds data for `x` and `y`. These values are mapped one-to-one in such a way that `x['Toyota Camry']` gets `y[0]` or `y[12.35]`.

6. For the `seriesStyles` property, we set the gradient color as `"40-#BD0070-#718680"` and set the `opacity` value as `0.7`.

# Stacked bar chart (Simple)

A stacked bar chart is a graph that is used to compare the parts that make up the whole. Each bar in the chart or graph is divided into other groupings, classifications, or combinations.

## Getting ready

Assuming we want to compare the sex ratios of males and females in certain sports, we could have them as follows:

- Bar A (Soccer): Boys 75% | Girls 25%
- Bar B (Tennis): Boys 50% | 50%
- Bar C (Swimming): Boys 45% | Girls 55%

The preceding statistics can be represented in a stacked bar chart. It is important to note that the major difference between a stacked and a regular bar chart is the `seriesList` property or option. Secondly, there's the addition of a new Boolean option called `stacked`, which should be set to `true`.

In an attempt to represent the preceding analytics via a Wijmo widget, we are going to modify our main code's `document ready` function as follows:

```
$(document).ready(function () {
        $("#wijbarchart").wijbarchart({
        stacked: true, //making a stacked bar chart
        axis: { //set up the x and y axes text and labels
            y: {
                text: "Engagement Ratio",

            },
            x: {
                text: "",
                labels: {
                    style: {
                        rotation: -45
                    }
                }
            }
        },
```

```
                hint: { //text to display on hover of chart
                    content: function () { //returns the label and y
    position
                        return this.data.label + '\n ' + this.y + '';
                    }
                },

                header: { //title of chart
                    text: "US Sports Engagement Ratio"
                },

                seriesList: [{ //seriesList stores label and corresponding
    data
                    label: "Soccer",
                    legendEntry: true,
                    data: { x: ['Boys', 'Girls'], y: [75, 25] }
                },{
                    label: "Tennis",
                    legendEntry: true,
                    data: { x: ['Boys', 'Girls'], y: [50, 50] }
                }, {
                    label: "Swimming",
                    legendEntry: true,
                        data: { x: ['Boys', 'Girls'], y: [45, 55] }
                }],


                seriesStyles: [{ //set fill colors for bar chart
                    fill: "#8ede43", stroke: "#7fc73c", opacity: 0.8
                }, {
                    fill: "#6aaba7", stroke: "#5f9996", opacity: 0.8
                }, {
                    fill: "#466a85", stroke: "#3e5f77", opacity: 0.8
                }],


                seriesHoverStyles: [{ "stroke-width": "1.5", opacity: 1
                }]
            });
        });
```

We updated the `seriesList` property of the `wijbarchart` object to contain the engagement ratio data for the boys and girls for each of the sports. If you successfully edit the code and run it, you'll have something like this:

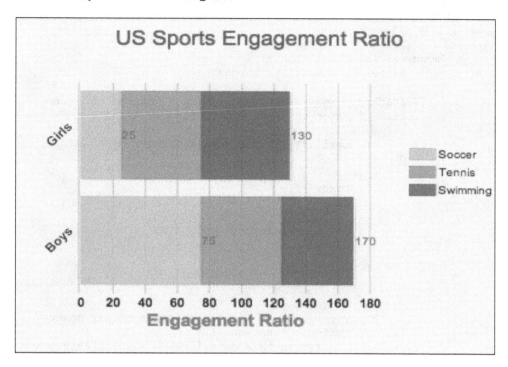

## How to do it...

1. We reference the Wijmo dependencies.

2. After the page loads, we set the `stacked` property to `true`.

3. The `x` and `y` properties are set, and `y` is rotated at `-45` degrees, which rotates the labels for boys and girls.

4. We set the `hint` property, which is displayed on hovering over the chart.

5. We set the `header` property, which is displayed atop the chart.

6. For the `seriesList` property, we have a `data` subproperty that holds data for `x` and `y`. These values are mapped one-to-one in such a way that `x['Boys']` gets `y[0]` or `y[75]`.

7. Note that the `stacked` option is set to `false` by default and updating it to `true` makes the `wijbarchart` object a stacked one.

## There's more...

To illustrate stacked bar charts with a more complex example, we are going to modify our original main code to create a stacked bar chart widget. Let's insert the following code snippet between our `script` tags:

```
$(document).ready(function () {
        $("#wijbarchart").wijbarchart({

        stacked: true, //ensures we have a stacked bar chart
        axis: { //set the text and labels for x and y axes
            y: {
                text: "Total Automobile Sales"
            },
            x: {
                text: "",
                labels: {
                    style: {
                        rotation: -45
                    }
                }
            }
        },

            hint: { //hint to display on hover of bar chart
                content: function () {
                    return this.data.label + '\n ' + this.y + '';
                }
            },

            header: { //bar chart title
                text: "US Toyota Automobile Statistics (Dummy
Data)"
            },

            seriesList: [{ //list of data, legend and label for
chart
                label: "US",
                legendEntry: true,
                data: { x: ['Toyota Camry', 'Toyota Corolla',
'Toyota Sienna'], y: [12.35, 21.50, 30.56] }
            }],
            seriesList: [{
                label: "US",
                legendEntry: true,
                data: { x: ['Toyota Camry', 'Toyota Corolla',
'Toyota Sienna'], y: [12.35, 21.50, 30.56] }
            }, {
                label: "Japan",
                legendEntry: true,
```

```
              data: { x: ['Toyota Camry', 'Toyota Corolla',
'Toyota Sienna'], y: [4.58, 1.23, 9.67] }
            }, {
                label: "Other",
                legendEntry: true,
                data: { x: ['Toyota Camry', 'Toyota Corolla',
'Toyota Sienna'], y: [31.59, 37.14, 65.32] }
            }],


        seriesStyles: [{ //fill color...
            fill: "#8ede43", stroke: "#7fc73c", opacity: 0.8
        }, {
            fill: "#6aaba7", stroke: "#5f9996", opacity: 0.8
        }, {
            fill: "#466a85", stroke: "#3e5f77", opacity: 0.8
        }],


        seriesHoverStyles: [{ "stroke-width": "1.5", opacity:
1
        }]
    });
});
```

When we run the preceding code after a proper insertion and successful formatting, we see a widget that looks similar to the following screenshot:

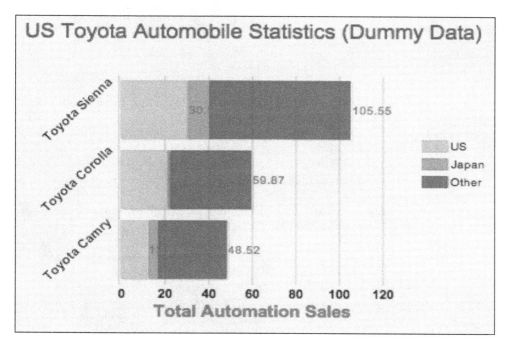

The preceding chart is what a stacked bar chart should look like, and this tells us how many Toyota cars were sold in the US, Japan, and other countries. However, as the title depicts, the chart focuses on US sales.

 The preceding chart compares the sales in the US, Japan, and other countries. Hence, we see that Toyota Sienna has the highest sales both in the US and overseas.

We can also see that Toyota Corolla has the lowest overall sales in Japan, and Toyota Sienna has its largest sales in other countries—quite a bit more than the sum of Sienna sales in the US and Japan.

# Animation and live data (Intermediate)

This recipe concentrates on a major and common widget for animations, known as the **wijexpander**. We will also see how to pass, handle, and manage live data via a Wijmo widget, which will in turn provide useful information to the users.

## Getting ready

The `wijexpander` object works in a way that allows the user to expand a bar or region, which could be a `div` HTML element, and have visibility into embedded web content such as a web page like CNN. We will see how to use the `wijexpander` object to display embedded web content via a given URL. Copy or recreate the following code:

```
<html>
<head>
<!--jQuery References-->
<script src="http://ajax.aspnetcdn.com/ajax/jquery/jquery-1.7.1.min.
js" type="text/javascript"></script>
<script src="http://ajax.aspnetcdn.com/ajax/jquery.ui/1.8.17/jquery-
ui.min.js" type="text/javascript"></script>
<!--Wijmo Widgets JavaScript-->
<script src="http://cdn.wijmo.com/jquery.wijmo-open.all.2.0.0.min.js"
type="text/javascript"></script>
<script src="http://cdn.wijmo.com/jquery.wijmo-complete.all.2.0.0.min.
js" type="text/javascript"></script>
<!--Theme-->
<link href="http://cdn.wijmo.com/themes/rocket/jquery-wijmo.css"
rel="stylesheet" type="text/css" title="rocket-jqueryui" />
<!--Wijmo Widgets CSS-->
<link href="http://cdn.wijmo.com/jquery.wijmo-complete.all.2.0.0.min.
css" rel="stylesheet" type="text/css" />
```

```
<style type="text/css">
    #my-wij-expander
    {
        width: 550px;
    }
    #webpage-content{
      height: 350px;
    }
</style>

</head>
<body>
<div id="my-wij-expander">
    <h3>cnn.com</h3>
    <div id="webpage-content"></div>
</div>

<script id="scriptInit" type="text/javascript">
    $(document).ready(function () {
        $("#my-wij-expander").wijexpander({
            contentUrl: "http://www.cnn.com",
            expandDirection: "top" //This expands the element
        });
    });
</script>
</html>
```

## How to do it...

1. First of all, we reference all the requisite code we need to run Wijmo.

2. Next, we create a `div` tag where the referenced URL content from CNN will be embedded.

3. Then, we create a script that instantiates a `wijexpander` widget by applying the necessary configurations for our expected expansion behavior and referencing the URL with which we intend to display its content.

4. Lastly, we add some basic styling to our content areas. If the code runs successfully, we should have a `wijexpander` object similar to the following screenshot:

5. Clicking on the expansion arrow will collapse the gray `div` area, thereby revealing the hidden URL content (CNN in this case) as follows:

▸ cnn.com

## There's more...

Here are a few other common options or configurations that would help you further customize your `wijexpander` widget:

▸ `disabled`: This option determines whether to disable or enable the behavior of the widget. If set to `false`, the widget becomes enabled. An example is shown as follows:

```
$("#myPrivateElement").wijexpander({ disabled: true });
```

▸ `expandDirection`: This option determines the direction that the content will expand to, as used in the preceding code. The available options for this property are `top`, `left`, `right`, and `bottom`. An example is shown as follows:

```
$("#my-wij-expander").wijexpander({ expandDirection: "left"
});
```

Wijmo expanders also have events and callbacks that are activated before and/or after certain events. For more information on `wijexpander` widgets, visit the following link:

`http://wijmo.com/wiki/index.php/Expander`

## Live data

Wijmo has claimed that all their charts have been optimized to support live data streaming. Data routinely gets fed into the widgets at any given frequency. This data automatically and continually recalculates and, subsequently, redraws the chart to convey useful desired information to the user. We will illustrate this using a Wijmo line chart, which displays information as a series of data points connected by straight point segments.

Enter the following code into your favorite code editor:

```html
<html>
<head>
<!--jQuery References-->
<script src="http://ajax.aspnetcdn.com/ajax/jquery/jquery-1.7.1.min.
js" type="text/javascript"></script>
<script src="http://ajax.aspnetcdn.com/ajax/jquery.ui/1.8.17/jquery-
ui.min.js" type="text/javascript"></script>
<!--Wijmo Widgets JavaScript-->
<script src="http://cdn.wijmo.com/jquery.wijmo-open.all.2.0.0.min.js"
type="text/javascript"></script>
<script src="http://cdn.wijmo.com/jquery.wijmo-complete.all.2.0.0.min.
js" type="text/javascript"></script>
<!--Theme-->
<link href="http://cdn.wijmo.com/themes/rocket/jquery-wijmo.css"
rel="stylesheet" type="text/css" title="rocket-jqueryui" />
<!--Wijmo Widgets CSS-->
<link href="http://cdn.wijmo.com/jquery.wijmo-complete.all.2.0.0.min.
css" rel="stylesheet" type="text/css" />
<script id="scriptInit" type="text/javascript">
        var myX = [], myY = [];
        var randomValuesCount = 10;
        var duration = 3000;
        var dx = 0;
        var intervalRandomData = null;

        $(document).ready(function () {
            for (dx = 0; dx < randomValuesCount; dx++) {
                myX.push(dx);
//random Y data points
                myY.push(createRandomValue());
            }
        //Instantiating the wijlinechart on #wijlinechart
            $("#wijlinechart").wijlinechart({
                showChartLabels: false,
                width: 700,
```

```
                    height: 425,
                    shadow: false,
                    animation: {
                        enabled: false
                    },
                    seriesTransition: {
                        enabled: false
                    },
                    legend: { visible: false },
                    hint: { enable: false },
                    header: { text: "Wijmo Live Data Simulation" },
                    axis:
                    {
                        y: { min: 0, max: 100, autoMin:false, autoMax:
false }
                    },
//creating the data points for the chart
                    seriesList: [
                        {
                            data: {
                                x: myX,
                                y: myY
                            },
                            markers: {
                                visible: true,
                                type: "circle"
                            }
                        }
                    ],
                    seriesStyles: [{ "stroke-width": 3, stroke:
"#00a6dd"}],

                    seriesHoverStyles: [{ "stroke-width": 4}]

                });

                doAnimate();

                intervalRandomData = setInterval(function () {
                    $("#wijlinechart").wijlinechart("addSeriesPoint", 0, {
x: dx++, y: createRandomValue() }, true); //keep adding points to the
series
                    doAnimate();
                }, duration);
            });

        function doAnimate() {
                var path = $("#wijlinechart").wijlinechart("getLinePath",
0), //handle to the path
                    markers = $("#wijlinechart").
wijlinechart("getLineMarkers", 0), //handle to the markers
```

```
                box = path.getBBox(),
                width = $("#wijlinechart").wijlinechart("option",
"width") / 10,
                anim = Raphael.animation({transform: Raphael.
format("...t{0},0", -width)}, duration); //how we want to animate. The
animation mechanism is referenced by variable anim.
            path.animate(anim); //animate the path using anim.
            if (path.shadow) {
                var pathShadow = path.shadow;
                pathShadow.animate(anim);
            }
            markers.animate(anim); //without this line, the markers
will not animate or move along with the path. We also want to animate
the markers using anim.
            var rect = box.x + " " + (box.y - 5) + " " + box.width + " "
+ (box.height + 10); //Comment A
            path.wijAttr("clip-rect", rect); //Comment B
            markers.attr("clip-rect", rect); //Comment C
            //Comments A, B, and C code lines prevent the line chart
animation from going outside the chart.
        }

        function createRandomValue() {
            var val = Math.round(Math.random() * 100);
            return val;
        }

    </script>
    </head>
    <body>
    <div>
        <div>
            <h2>Streaming Live Random Data</h2>
        </div>
        <div class="main">
            <div id="wijlinechart"></div>
            <div class="demo-options"></div>
        </div>
        <div class="footer">
            <p>
        This demo simulates streaming live randomized data using the
<u>getLinePath</u> and <u>getLineMarkers</u> methods.
            </p>
        </div>
    </div>
</body>
</html>
```

If the preceding code runs successfully, we should have an animated chart that looks like this:

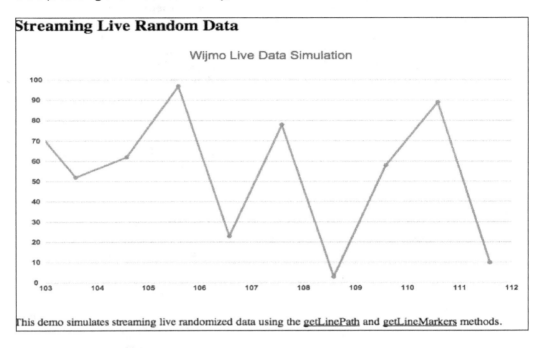

This demo simulates streaming live randomized data using the getLinePath and getLineMarkers methods.

The preceding code that generated this animation is properly commented to give reasons as to why certain lines were coded the way they were. In a nutshell, anyone could customize the code to stream live data from a server or a constantly-fed spreadsheet or XML data, using the JavaScript calls within certain timed intervals. The JavaScript function setInterval() is also pretty helpful in achieving this.

 The preceding code is similar to the one found at http://wijmo.com/demo/explore/?widget=LineChart&sample=Streaming%20data.

# Bubble chart (Intermediate)

A bubble chart is a chart whose data points are replaced with bubbles of various shapes and scattered across the chart. It is like a scatter chart. The Wijmo widget representing a bubble chart is referred to as a `wijbubblechart` object.

## Getting ready

The data points or bubbles each have three non-dependent values, x, y, and y1 as follows:

- The value x defines the Cartesian position along the x axis
- The value y defines the Cartesian position along the y axis
- The value y1 defines the bubble size at each point

Having understood a bubble chart and the three values that define the positions of the bubble, we can now happily proceed with an implementation. Let us create a `wijbubblechart` object of the percentage of college graduates in six major cities around the world. This is dummy data and doesn't reflect the actual relationship between college graduates and the health of the corresponding economy. However, this dummy data is based on the assumption that a city with more graduates per thousand will have a smarter economy. Also, this depends on the overall population of that city.

Enter the following code into your favorite code editor:

```
<html>
<head>
<!--jQuery References-->
<script src="http://ajax.aspnetcdn.com/ajax/jquery/jquery-1.7.1.min.
js" type="text/javascript"></script>
<script src="http://ajax.aspnetcdn.com/ajax/jquery.ui/1.8.17/jquery-
ui.min.js" type="text/javascript"></script>
<!--Wijmo Widgets JavaScript-->
<script src="http://cdn.wijmo.com/jquery.wijmo-open.all.2.0.0.min.js"
type="text/javascript"></script>
<script src="http://cdn.wijmo.com/jquery.wijmo-complete.all.2.0.0.min.
js" type="text/javascript"></script>
<!--Theme-->
<link href="http://cdn.wijmo.com/themes/rocket/jquery-wijmo.css"
rel="stylesheet" type="text/css" title="rocket-jqueryui" />
<!--Wijmo Widgets CSS-->
<link href="http://cdn.wijmo.com/jquery.wijmo-complete.all.2.0.0.min.
css" rel="stylesheet" type="text/css" />

<script type="text/javascript">
        $(document).ready(function () {
```

```
$("#myWijbubblechart").wijbubblechart({
    showChartLabels: false,
    axis: {
        y: {
            text: "Smart Economy Rating"
        },
        x: {
            text: "College Graduates(Per Thousand)"
        }
    },
    hint: {
        content: function () {
            return this.data.label;
        }
    },
    header: {
        text: "College Graduates Vs. Health of the Economy
- 2012"
    },
    seriesList: [{
        label: "Beijing",
        legendEntry: true,
        data: { y: [85], x: [150], y1: [1340] },
        markers: {
            type: "tri"
        }
    }, {
        label: "New Delhi",
        legendEntry: true,
        data: { y: [80], x: [167], y1: [1150] },
        markers: {
            type: "diamond"
        }
    }, {
        label: "Los Angeles",
        legendEntry: true,
        data: { y: [92], x: [400], y1: [309] },
        markers: {
            type: "circle"
        }
    }, {
        label: "Tokyo",
        legendEntry: true,
        data: { y: [94], x: [250], y1: [126] },
        markers: {
            type: "invertedTri"
        }
    }, {
        label: "London",
        legendEntry: true,
```

```
                    data: { y: [82], x: [200], y1: [140] },
                    markers: {
                         type: "cross"
                    }
               }, {
                    label: "Lagos",
                    legendEntry: true,
                    data: { y: [48], x: [374], y1: [72] },
                    markers: {
                         type: "box"
                    }
               }]
          });
     });
</script>
</head>

<body>
<div id="myWijbubblechart" class="ui-widget ui-widget-content ui-
corner-all" style="width: 500px;
height: 300px">
</div>
</body>
</html>
```

If the preceding code is copied correctly and run in a browser, we should have a Wijmo bubble chart similar to the following screenshot:

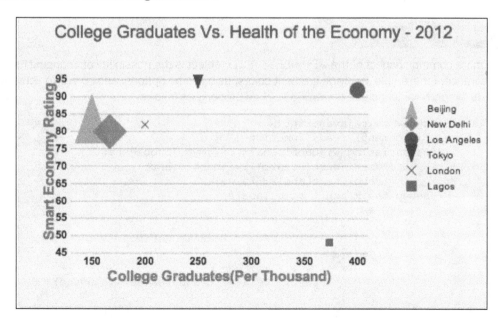

## How to do it...

1. To see how the `wijbubblechart` object works, we can simply examine one of the objects in the `seriesList` property, like this one:

```
{
        label: "Beijing",
        legendEntry: true,
        data: { y: [85], x: [150], y1: [1340] },
        markers: {
            type: "tri"
        }
    },
```

2. Remember that we already defined `x`, `y`, and `y1` as the values of a point on the x axis, a point on the y axis, and the size of the bubble respectively. So in this case, for Beijing the value for `y` is set to `85`, and the size of the bubble, `y1`, is `1340`. The `legendEntry` property is set to `true` so we can see Beijing in the legend area by the right of the chart.

3. We can see the various bubbles in different shapes and a legend that tells what city each bubble represents. The `type` property of the `markers` object is responsible for setting the shape of the bubble.

```
markers: {
        type: "tri"
    }
```

## There's more...

One more common aspect of the `wijbubblechart` object is the possibility of changing its appearance, for example, applying gradient colors, using some options, and so on. To achieve this we simply have to include a `seriesStyles` property as follows:

```
<script type="text/javascript">
        $(document).ready(function () {
    //instantiating wijbubblechart on #myWijbubblechart
            $("#myWijbubblechart").wijbubblechart({
                showChartLabels: false,
    //setup the x and y axis labels
                axis: {
                    y: {
                        text: "Smart Economy Rating"
                    },
                    x: {
                        text: "College Graduates (Per Thousand)"
                    }
                },
    //Display hint text on chart hover
```

```
                    hint: {
                        content: function () {
                            return this.data.label;
                        }
                    },
        //title of chart
                    header: {
                        text: "College Graduates Vs. Health of the Economy
    - 2012"
                    },
        //chart color fill styles
                    seriesStyles: [{
                fill: "180-#8F8F8F-#C462AC", stroke: "#8F8F8F"
                }, {
                fill: "45-#C462AC-#2371B0", stroke: "#C462AC"
                }, {
                fill: "90-#4A067D-#0B7D19", stroke: "#4A067D"
                }, {
                fill: "270-#2371B0-#6AABA7", stroke: "#2371B0"
                }, {
                fill: "45-#0C85F0-#852E85", stroke: "#0C85F0"
                }, {
                fill: "180-#6AABA7-#AB6A9C", stroke: "#6AABA7"
                }],
        //data values for each bubble
                    seriesList: [{
                        label: "Beijing",
                        legendEntry: true,
                        data: { y: [85], x: [150], y1: [1340] },
                        markers: {
                            type: "tri"
                        }
                    }, {
                        label: "New Delhi",
                        legendEntry: true,
                        data: { y: [80], x: [167], y1: [1150] },
                        markers: {
                            type: "diamond"
                        }
                    }, {
                        label: "Los Angeles",
                        legendEntry: true,
                        data: { y: [92], x: [400], y1: [309] },
                        markers: {
                            type: "circle"
                        }
                    }, {
                        label: "Tokyo",
                        legendEntry: true,
                        data: { y: [94], x: [250], y1: [126] },
```

```
                    markers: {
                        type: "invertedTri"
                    }
                }, {
                    label: "London",
                    legendEntry: true,
                    data: { y: [82], x: [200], y1: [140] },
                    markers: {
                        type: "cross"
                    }
                }, {
                    label: "Lagos",
                    legendEntry: true,
                    data: { y: [48], x: [374], y1: [72] },
                    markers: {
                        type: "box"
                    }
                }]
            });
        });
    </script>
```

 The `script` tags should be embedded within the HTML tags for a successful run.

If we successfully run the preceding code, we should have a bubble chart that looks like this:

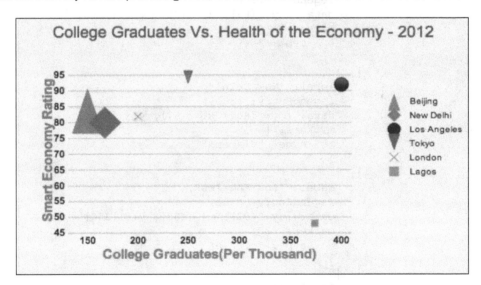

You can visit `http://wijmo.com/wiki/index.php/Bubblechart` for more details about Wijmo bubble charts and more advanced options available for customizing your charts.

# Calendar (Intermediate)

The calendar Wijmo widget, referred to as **wijcalendar**, is one of the most straightforward widgets available. The `wijcalendar` object is a Wijmo calendar with customizable properties and configurations.

## How to do it...

1. Here's a simple code that will generate a `wijcalendar` object:

```html
<html>
<head>
<!--jQuery References-->
<script src="http://ajax.aspnetcdn.com/ajax/jquery/jquery-
1.7.1.min.js" type="text/javascript"></script>
<script src="http://ajax.aspnetcdn.com/ajax/jquery.ui/1.8.17/
jquery-ui.min.js" type="text/javascript"></script>
<!--Wijmo Widgets JavaScript-->
<script src="http://cdn.wijmo.com/jquery.wijmo-open.all.2.0.0.min.
js" type="text/javascript"></script>
<script src="http://cdn.wijmo.com/jquery.wijmo-complete.
all.2.0.0.min.js" type="text/javascript"></script>
<!--Theme-->
<link href="http://cdn.wijmo.com/themes/rocket/jquery-wijmo.css"
rel="stylesheet" type="text/css" title="rocket-jqueryui" />
<!--Wijmo Widgets CSS-->
<link href="http://cdn.wijmo.com/jquery.wijmo-complete.
all.2.0.0.min.css" rel="stylesheet" type="text/css" />
<script type="text/javascript">
        $(function () {
            $("#myWijCalendar").wijcalendar(
                { easing: "easeInQuad" }
            );
        });
</script>
<body>
<div id="myWijCalendar" class="ui-widget ui-widget-content ui-
corner-all" style="width: 500px;height: 300px">
</div>
</body>
</html>
```

2. From the preceding script we target the `#myWijCalendar` object in the DOM, and call `wijcalendar`, which initializes the calendar widget and supplies `"easeInQuad"` to the easing property.

3. Assuming there are no mistakes in the code, we should have a calendar widget that is similar to this:

## See also

For a list of common options that will help customize the `wijcalendar` object further, visit `http://wijmo.com/wiki/index.php/Calendar`.

# Grids (Advanced)

A grid, in general, is similar to an Excel spreadsheet with headers per column and corresponding data per row or tuple. Customizations, edits, selections, and other forms of manipulations, such as calculations, can be carried out directly on the spreadsheet. Usually, such spreadsheets are used to gather information regarding a specific thing or event. The purpose of these grids is to visualize the relationships and correlation between data and, subsequently, to provide valuable information.

The `wijgrid` object is instantiated or, rather, created by the `jquery.wijmo.wijgrid.js` library.

## Getting ready

First and foremost, `wijgrid` objects are dependent on the `<table>` HTML tag in a given document. So, we need to create a table and host our grid widget, the `wijgrid` object, on it. Here's one example of how to create a table in HTML:

```
//Example 1:
<table>
  <thead>
    <th>column0 Header</th>
    <th>column1 Header</th>
  </thead>
  <tbody></tbody>
</table>
```

Don't forget to wrap the preceding table code with the `<html>` and `<body>` tags.

Now that we have the table, we need to target it and host the `wijgrid` object on it. We can target any table in a given HTML document via jQuery as seen in the following example:

```
//Example 2:
$("table").wijgrid({
    data: [[0, "x"], [1, "y"], [2, "z"]]
});
```

Successfully running the preceding snippets of code, `Example 1` and `Example 2`, will draw or display a Wijmo grid on your browser, having two columns and three rows similar to the following screenshot:

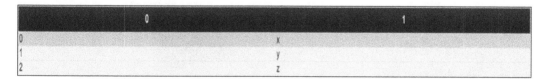

## How to do it...

The code in `Example 2` is the proper syntax for creating or hosting a `wijgrid` object on a table. The `data` property of the `wijgrid` function is an array with three data points. Each data point is an array, `[0, "x"]`, `[1, "y"]`, and `[2, "z"]`. The array count, or length for each array, signifies that we are going to have a grid with two columns and three (total number of arrays in `data`) rows, excluding the header. It is important to note that the table structure is only a framework for Wijmo to run on. Hence, the texts defined in the preceding `<th>` tags never get rendered. Wijmo parses these arrays by looking at the number of arrays in `data`, accounting for three rows, and each array in `data` being a row as follows:

▸ Each array represents a row on the grid

▸ Each data point in each array represents data for each column in the grid

Wijmo parses data and is quickly able to draw the resulting grid on your page, as seen in the preceding section.

1. Now let's use a better real-life example, incorporating all the Wijmo dependencies. Assume we have a group called "City Devs without Borders", and we want to create a grid of three people whose works have been significant in improving the security in Gotham city. We want a list of their names, dates of birth, and occupations in tabular format, which is best represented by a `wijgrid` object.

2. Type this code in your favorite editor:

```html
<html>
<head>
<!--jQuery References-->
<script src="http://ajax.aspnetcdn.com/ajax/jquery/jquery-
1.7.1.min.js" type="text/javascript"></script>
<script src="http://ajax.aspnetcdn.com/ajax/jquery.ui/1.8.17/
jquery-ui.min.js" type="text/javascript"></script>
<!--Wijmo Widgets JavaScript-->
<script src="http://cdn.wijmo.com/jquery.wijmo-open.all.2.0.0.min.
js" type="text/javascript"></script>
<script src="http://cdn.wijmo.com/jquery.wijmo-complete.
all.2.0.0.min.js" type="text/javascript"></script>
<!--Theme-->
<link href="http://cdn.wijmo.com/themes/rocket/jquery-wijmo.css"
rel="stylesheet" type="text/css" title="rocket-jqueryui" />
<!--Wijmo Widgets CSS-->
<link href="http://cdn.wijmo.com/jquery.wijmo-complete.
all.2.0.0.min.css" rel="stylesheet" type="text/css" />
</head>
<body>
<table>
  <thead>
    <th>column0</th>
    <th>column1</th>
  </thead>
  <tbody>

  </tbody>
</table>

<script type="text/javascript">
var columns = [
    { headerText: 'First Name', dataKey: 'firstName', dataType:
'string'},
    { headerText: 'Last Name', dataKey: 'lastName', dataType:
'string' },
```

```
    { headerText: 'Date of Birth', dateKey: 'DOB', dataType:
'string' },
    { headerText: 'Occupation', dataKey: 'occupation', dataType:
'string' }
];
var content = [
    {
        firstName: 'Tochi',
        lastName: 'Eke-Okoro',
        DOB: '08/21',
        occupation: 'UI Developer'
    },
    {

        firstName: 'Ryan',
        lastName: 'Krest',
        DOB: '06/1',
        occupation: 'Attorney'
    },
    {
        firstName: 'Bruce',
        lastName: 'Romeo',
        DOB: '02/26',
        occupation: 'US Navy'
    }
];
$("table").wijgrid({
    columns: columns,
    data: content
});
</script>
</body>
</html>
```

3. Running the preceding code successfully will render a widget similar to this:

| First Name | Last Name | Date of Birth | Occupation |
|---|---|---|---|
| Tochi | Eke-Okoro | 08/21 | UI Developer |
| Ryan | Krest | 06/1 | Attorney |
| Bruce | Romeo | 02/26 | US Navy |

Again, here's a stepwise workflow of how the preceding `wijgrid` object was created in a nutshell:

1. Create an HTML table for `wijgrid` to hook on to.

2. Create the columns and content to populate the grid. The column is an optional property of `wijgrid`, which is an array of column objects. A column object also has optional properties, such as `headerText`, which holds the string for the column header name; `dataKey`, which maps the column to a content property, such as `firstName`; and `dataType`, which is the data's type, such as `string`, `dateTime`, or `number`.

3. Create the content. The content is an array of objects. Each object corresponds to the data for each row. Also, the column's `dataKey` property is usually mapped to one of the content properties.

4. Finally, target the table and host the `wijgrid` object on it. Set the `wijgrid` object's data option to our created content array. Also set the `wijgrid` object's `columns` property to our created `columns` array.

5. Run the code to draw the `wijgrid` object.

## There's more...

The `wijgrid` object provides options that add customizable features and functionalities to the grid. Some of these functionalities include things such as editing the grid via a simple click of the button, adding a row to the top of the grid, and adding a row of data to the bottom of the grid. Using JavaScript events, we can achieve this by listening to, say, a button being clicked.

Using the same example used previously, we are going to write functions to do the following:

▸ Change the first name on the first row of the grid by clicking a button

▸ Prepend a row of data to the top of the grid by clicking a button

▸ Append a row of data to the bottom of the grid by clicking a button

Copy the following complete code into your editor:

```html
<html>
<head>
<!--jQuery References-->
<script src="http://ajax.aspnetcdn.com/ajax/jquery/jquery-1.7.1.min.
js" type="text/javascript"></script>
<script src="http://ajax.aspnetcdn.com/ajax/jquery.ui/1.8.17/jquery-
ui.min.js" type="text/javascript"></script>
<!--Wijmo Widgets JavaScript-->
<script src="http://cdn.wijmo.com/jquery.wijmo-open.all.2.0.0.min.js"
type="text/javascript"></script>
<script src="http://cdn.wijmo.com/jquery.wijmo-complete.all.2.0.0.min.
js" type="text/javascript"></script>
```

```
<!--Theme-->
<link href="http://cdn.wijmo.com/themes/rocket/jquery-wijmo.css"
rel="stylesheet" type="text/css" title="rocket-jqueryui" />
<!--Wijmo Widgets CSS-->
<link href="http://cdn.wijmo.com/jquery.wijmo-complete.all.2.0.0.min.
css" rel="stylesheet" type="text/css" />
</head>
<body>
<table>
  <thead>
    <th>column0</th>
    <th>column1</th>
  </thead>
  <tbody>

  </tbody>
</table><p></p>
<button style="clear:both;" id="btnUpdate">Update First Name</
button> 
<button style="clear:both;" id="btnPrepend">Add Row to Grid Top</
button> 
<button style="clear:both;" id="btnAppend">Add Row to Grid Bottom</
button>
<script type="text/javascript">
var columns = [
    { headerText: 'First Name', dataKey: 'firstName', dataType:
'string'},
    { headerText: 'Last Name', dataKey: 'lastName', dataType: 'string'
},
    { headerText: 'Date of Birth', dateKey: 'DOB', dataType: 'string'
},
    { headerText: 'Occupation', dataKey: 'occupation', dataType:
'string' }
];
var content = [
    {
        firstName: 'Tochi',
        lastName: 'Eke-Okoro',
        DOB: '08/21',
        occupation: 'UI Developer'
    },
    {

        firstName: 'Ryan',
        lastName: 'Krest',
        DOB: '06/1',
        occupation: 'Attorney'
    },
    {
```

```
            firstName: 'Bruce',
            lastName: 'Romeo',
            DOB: '02/26',
            occupation: 'US Navy'
      }
  ];
  $("table").wijgrid({
      columns: columns,
      data: content
  });

    var newPerson = {

        firstName: 'Empty firstname to update later',
        lastName: 'Empty lastname to update later',
        DOB: (new Date).toString(),
        occupation: 'Empty occupation to update later'
      }

  var $obj = $("table");
  $("#btnUpdate").click(function() {

      data = $obj.wijgrid("data");
      if(data[0].firstName == "Mije")
        alert('SORRY!! First name already set to Mije') ;
      data[0].firstName = "Mije";
      $obj.wijgrid("ensureControl", true);

  });

  $("#btnPrepend").click(function() {
      data = $obj.wijgrid("data");
      data.unshift(newPerson); //prepend data or object to array
      $obj.wijgrid("ensureControl", true);
  });

  $("#btnAppend").click(function() {
      data = $obj.wijgrid("data");
      data.push(newPerson); //append data or object to array
      $obj.wijgrid("ensureControl", true);
  });

  </script>
  </body>
  </html>
```

If the preceding code is run successfully on your browser, after pressing one of the buttons you will see a Wijmo grid similar to the following screenshot:

| First Name | Last Name | Date of Birth | Occupation |
|---|---|---|---|
| Empty firstname to update later | Empty lastname to update later | Thu Dec 20 2012 18:54:32 GMT-0500 (EST) | Empty occupation to update later |
| Empty firstname to update later | Empty lastname to update later | Thu Dec 20 2012 18:54:32 GMT-0500 (EST) | Empty occupation to update later |
| Empty firstname to update later | Empty lastname to update later | Thu Dec 20 2012 18:54:32 GMT-0500 (EST) | Empty occupation to update later |
| Mije | Eke-Okoro | 08/21 | UI Developer |
| Ryan | Krest | 06/1 | Attorney |
| Bruce | Romeo | 02/26 | US Navy |
| Empty firstname to update later | Empty lastname to update later | Thu Dec 20 2012 18:54:32 GMT-0500 (EST) | Empty occupation to update later |
| Empty firstname to update later | Empty lastname to update later | Thu Dec 20 2012 18:54:32 GMT-0500 (EST) | Empty occupation to update later |
| Empty firstname to update later | Empty lastname to update later | Thu Dec 20 2012 18:54:32 GMT-0500 (EST) | Empty occupation to update later |

| Update First Name | Add Row to Grid Top | Add Row to Grid Bottom |
|---|---|---|

Let us go through the code one more time, focusing on the differences between it and the previous static `wijgrid` void of buttons.

- Clicking on the **Update First Name** button will always update the first name in the first row to **Mije,** and if it is already set to **Mije**, it will alert the **SORRY** message.

- Clicking on the **Add Row to Grid Top** button will prepend the dummy data, programmatically referenced by `newPerson`, to the `wijgrid` object. The `newPerson` object contains data for each column, including the date of birth, which in this case has been defaulted to the entry date (now) of this row, captured in `new Date`. For future programming exercises, or self-supervised tryouts, you could try writing functions to edit each cell of the row.

- Clicking on the **Add Row to Grid Bottom** button will append the dummy data (the same dummy data mentioned previously), referenced by `newPerson`, to the `wijgrid` object.

- The `$obj.wijgrid("ensureControl", true)` object ensures that we have the permission to control the Wijmo grid, else we won't see or notice any changes when the buttons are clicked.

Now we know how to edit the `wijgrid` object by writing functions that trigger those updates when certain events occur, for example, the click of a button. Let us see a pretty hassle-free way of editing the grid right on `wijgrid` itself. This is similar to editing the cell just like you would in an Excel spreadsheet, by double-clicking on it.

Change the preceding code to the following:

```
$("table").wijgrid({
    columns: columns,
    data: content,
    allowEditing: true
});
```

This will make every cell editable by simply double-clicking on it. Here is a list of cool options to further customize your `wijgrid` object:

```
$("#table").wijgrid({ allowKeyboardNavigation: true}); //allows
keyboard navigation
$("#table").wijgrid({ allowPaging: true}); //allows pagination on
wijgrid
$("#table").wijgrid({ allowSorting: true}); //allows wijgrid to be
sorted
$("#table").wijgrid({ culture: "en"}); //sets the culture ID of the
wijgrid
$("#table").wijgrid({ loadingText: "I'm Loading…"}); //sets the
loading text
```

## See also

▸   Visit `http://wijmo.com/wiki/index.php/Grid` for more information about Wijmo grids

# Data source (Advanced)

Wijmo provides a class for accessing data via a `datareader` object and an optional proxy parameter. The data could be stored locally via a specific format, and parsed via a `datareader` object. The proxy property holds the URL to the service that renders or holds the required data, which is usually in the backend and not stored on the client side.

We refer to this class as the `wijdatasource` class. The `jquery.wijmo.wijdatasource.js` library is responsible for creating the `wijdatasource` widget class and it contains two sample proxy and reader classes.

## Getting ready

Assume we want to parse or simply display a list of a few popular cities of the world, and that this data will be created and stored locally in our widget as follows:

```
var testArr = ["London", "Brussels", "Los Angeles", "Abuja",
"Johannesburg", "Paris", "Amsterdam"];
```

To create our `List of major cities` app, we can initialize a `wijdatasource` class and utilize our data as follows:

```
<html>
<head>
<title>List of major cities app!! </title>
<!--jQuery References-->
<script src="http://ajax.aspnetcdn.com/ajax/jquery/jquery-1.7.1.min.
```

```
js" type="text/javascript"></script>
<script src="http://ajax.aspnetcdn.com/ajax/jquery.ui/1.8.17/jquery-
ui.min.js" type="text/javascript"></script>
<!--Wijmo Widgets JavaScript-->
<script src="http://cdn.wijmo.com/jquery.wijmo-open.all.2.0.0.min.js"
type="text/javascript"></script>
<script src="http://cdn.wijmo.com/jquery.wijmo-complete.all.2.0.0.min.
js" type="text/javascript"></script>
<!--Theme-->
<link href="http://cdn.wijmo.com/themes/rocket/jquery-wijmo.css"
rel="stylesheet" type="text/css" title="rocket-jqueryui" />
<!--Wijmo Widgets CSS-->
<link href="http://cdn.wijmo.com/jquery.wijmo-complete.all.2.0.0.min.
css" rel="stylesheet" type="text/css" />
</head>
<body>
<span><h5>Hi Folks!! </h5></span>
<span>This app prints nothing to screen but logs the local data read
via datareader to console...</span>

<script type="text/javascript">
// array to read {List of popular cities around the world...}
var testArr = ["London", "Brussels", "Los Angeles", "Abuja",
"Johannesburg", "Paris", "Amsterdam"];
// create datareader of array
var myReader = new wijarrayreader([{name: 'label'}, {name: 'value'},
{name: 'selected',defaultValue: false}]);
// create datasource

var datasource = new wijdatasource({
    reader: myReader,
    data: testArr,
    loaded: function (data){
              // get items by data.items
              console.log(data.items)

          }
});
// load datasource, loaded event will be fired after loading.
datasource.load();
</script>
</body>
</html>
```

If the code is successfully run, you will see a message on your browser's screen telling you what the app does. A log of the objects is outputted to the console.

## How to do it...

1. Once again, we add references to the Wijmo widget dependency files from CDN.

2. Next, we create the list of cities.

3. Next, we create the `datareader` object that has the format for arranging our list, and we set the `datareader` object to a `myReader` handle.

4. Time for the real deal! We initialize the `datasource` object as follows:

```
var datasource = new wijdatasource({
    reader: myReader,
    data: testArr,
    loaded: function (data){
            // get items by data.items
            console.log(data.items)

        }
});
```

5. Then, we load the `datasource` object using `datasource.load()`. The `loaded` function, which is a property of `wijdatasource`, is called after `datasource.load()` fires off. The loaded data is referenced as the parameter or argument in that function for which the items within can be referenced by `data.items`.

It is also possible to load data from a prepared `datasource` object into a targeted UI element such as a `<div>` or `<p>` tag. This `datasource` object could be prepared via a proxy, which is a mechanism for retrieving data from a remote source, or locally as previously shown.

To show how to work with `wijdatasource` and HTML elements, let us look at one more example that utilizes local data. Assume that we have a list of some countries we want to populate in a list. Assume that we also want a selection of those cities visible only after some substring of that country is entered in an input field. We also want this event to trigger only when a button is clicked.

For instance, say we have a list containing the words *Computer*, *Motherboard*, *Commute*, *Mother*, *apple*, and *people*. If the user enters `Com` and clicks on the button, the output should be a new list containing `Computer` and `Commute`. Also, if the user enters `ple` and clicks on the button, the output should be a new list containing `apple` and `people`.

To properly illustrate this, we will make use of a Wijmo widget called `wijlist`. A `wijlist` object is simply a Wijmo list widget, which can be created by targeting a given element on the page and initiating the widget on it with the following code:

```
var myArr = [6,7,8,9,0];
$('.myList').wijlist('setItems', myArr);
//Render the list in the client browser
list.wijlist('renderList');
```

The preceding code assumes the existence of a class called `myList`, and we initialize or host the `wijlist` object on all elements with a `myList` class. We create a local array referenced by `myArr`. Finally, we render the `wijlist` object on our browser.

Having understood what a `wijlist` object is and how to deploy one in our widget, we can proceed with our app. Enter the following code in your favorite editor:

```
<!--jQuery References-->
<html>
<head>
<script src="http://ajax.aspnetcdn.com/ajax/jquery/jquery-1.7.1.min.
js" type="text/javascript"></script>
<script src="http://ajax.aspnetcdn.com/ajax/jquery.ui/1.8.17/jquery-
ui.min.js" type="text/javascript"></script>
<!--Wijmo Widgets JavaScript-->
<script src="http://cdn.wijmo.com/jquery.wijmo-open.all.2.0.0.min.js"
type="text/javascript"></script>
<script src="http://cdn.wijmo.com/jquery.wijmo-complete.all.2.0.0.min.
js" type="text/javascript"></script>
<!--Theme-->
<link href="http://cdn.wijmo.com/themes/rocket/jquery-wijmo.css"
rel="stylesheet" type="text/css" title="rocket-jqueryui" />
<!--Wijmo Widgets CSS-->
<link href="http://cdn.wijmo.com/jquery.wijmo-complete.all.2.0.0.min.
css" rel="stylesheet" type="text/css" />
</head>
<body>
<div class="ui-widget">
    <P>Enter either whole or part of any of the following words
(representing some countries): "United States of America", "United
Arab Emirates", "Australia", "Canada", "Luxembourg", "Granada",
"Nigeria" or "Niger", then click the Load Data button. Data that
matches the whole or part of the value you entered, will be loaded
into the wijlist.</p>
        <input style="width: 250px" id="testInput" type="textbox"
class="ui-widget-content ui-corner-all" />
        <input type="button" id="loadData" value="Load Data" />
    <div id="list" style="height: 300px; width: 400px;"></div>
</div>
<script>
 $(document).ready(function () {
        $("#list").wijlist({});
        var testArray = [{
                label: 'United States of America',
                value: 'United States of America'
            }, {
                label: 'United Arab Emirates',
                value: 'United Arab Emirates'
            }, {
```

```
                        label: 'Australia',
                        value: 'Australia'
                }, {
                        label: 'Canada',
                        value: 'Canada'
                }, {
                        label: 'Luxembourg',
                        value: 'Luxembourg'
                }, {
                        label: 'Granada',
                        value: 'Granada'
                }, {
                        label: 'Nigeria',
                        value: 'Nigeria'
                }, {
                        label: 'Niger',
                        value: 'Niger'
                }];
                loadList(testArray);
                $('input#loadData').click(function(){
                    var text = $('input#testInput').val().toLowerCase();
                    if(text == "" || text == null){
                        alert('No Match');
                        return ;
                    }
                    var matches = [];
                    for(var i = 0; i < testArray.length; i++){
                      var newTxt = testArray[i].label.toLowerCase();
                        if(newTxt.indexOf(text) > -1){
                            //console.log('found');
                            matches.push(testArray[i]);
                        }
                    }
                        loadList(matches)
                        return ;

                //console.log('failed');
                });
                function loadList(arr){
                        var list = $("#list");
                        //set the array testArray to the Wijmo list widget
                        list.wijlist('setItems', arr);
                        //Render the list in the client browser
                        list.wijlist('renderList');
                }

        });
        </script>
        </body>
        </html>
```

If the preceding code is successfully run, you will have something like this in your browser:

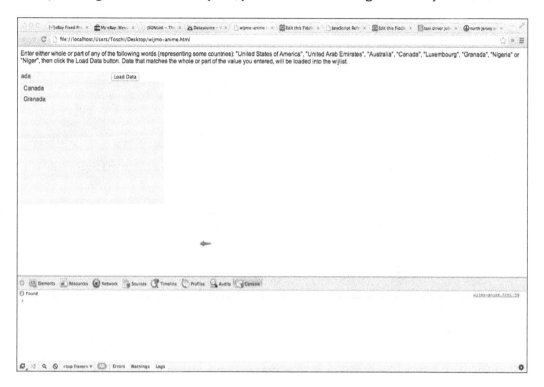

So once again, starting from the `document.ready` function, we will go through our code to explain how this widget works:

1. First of all, we create a `wijlist` object by hosting it on the `div` tag with `id = list`.

2. Next, we create a local array, `testArray`, which will be digested by the `loadList` function. This will set `testArray` as the new content of the `wijlist` object.

3. By clicking the **Load Data** button, we compare the text entered in the input field with `id = "testInput"`, and each of the items in the `wijlist` object via a `for` loop.

4. During the loop, we append subsequent matches to a new local array, `newList`.

5. At the end of the loop, if `newList` is not empty we set `newList` as the new Wijmo list data, thus overwriting the previous list data and getting a new result in our browser.

In the just-concluded example, it is important to note that we only used a local array without making reference to a `wijdatasource` object. Usually, some array is passed as one of the properties in the parameters of a `wijdatasource` object, which sets the array as a `datasource` object. The app we just created did not use a `datasource` object but a `wijlist` object.

To use the `datasource` and `wijlist` objects, copy the following code into your editor and run it:

```html
<!--jQuery References-->
<html>
<script src="http://ajax.aspnetcdn.com/ajax/jquery/jquery-1.7.1.min.
js" type="text/javascript"></script>
<script src="http://ajax.aspnetcdn.com/ajax/jquery.ui/1.8.17/jquery-
ui.min.js" type="text/javascript"></script>
<!--Wijmo Widgets JavaScript-->
<script src="http://cdn.wijmo.com/jquery.wijmo-open.all.2.0.0.min.js"
type="text/javascript"></script>
<script src="http://cdn.wijmo.com/jquery.wijmo-complete.all.2.0.0.min.
js" type="text/javascript"></script>
<!--Theme-->
<link href="http://cdn.wijmo.com/themes/rocket/jquery-wijmo.css"
rel="stylesheet" type="text/css" title="rocket-jqueryui" />
<!--Wijmo Widgets CSS-->
<link href="http://cdn.wijmo.com/jquery.wijmo-complete.all.2.0.0.min.
css" rel="stylesheet" type="text/css" />

<div class="ui-widget">
    <P>Enter either whole or part of any of the following words
(representing some countries): "United States of America", "United
Arab Emirates", "Australia", "Canada", "Luxembourg", "Granada",
"Nigeria" or "Niger", then click the Load Data button. Data that
matches the whole or part of the value you entered, will be loaded
into the wijlist.</p>
    <input style="width: 250px" id="testInput" type="textbox"
class="ui-widget-content ui-corner-all" />
    <input type="button" id="loadData" value="Load Data" />
    <div id="list" style="height: 300px; width: 400px;"></div>
</div>
<script>
 $(document).ready(function () {
        $("#list").wijlist({});
     var testArray = [{
             label: 'United States of America',
             value: 'United States of America'
         }, {
             label: 'United Arab Emirates',
             value: 'United Arab Emirates'
         }, {
             label: 'Australia',
             value: 'Australia'
         }, {
             label: 'Canada',
             value: 'Canada'
         }, {
             label: 'Luxembourg',
```

```
                    value: 'Luxembourg'
        }, {
            label: 'Granada',
            value: 'Granada'
        }, {
            label: 'Nigeria',
            value: 'Nigeria'
        }, {
            label: 'Niger',
            value: 'Niger'
    }];
    //var datasource = null;
    var myReader = new wijarrayreader([{name: 'label'}, {name:
'value'}, {name: 'selected',defaultValue: false}]);
        var datasource = new wijdatasource({
            reader: myReader,
            data: testArray,
            loaded: function (data){
                // get items by data.items
                loadList(data.items);


            }
        });
    datasource.load();
     function loadList(items){
        var list = $("#list");
        //set the array testArray to the Wijmo list widget
        list.wijlist('setItems', items);
        //Render the list in the client browser
        list.wijlist('renderList');


    }
    $('#loadData').click(function(){
      //process this section when the load Data is clicked...
      var text = $('input#testInput').val().toLowerCase();
        if(text == "" || text == null){
            alert('No Match');
            return ;
        }
      var newList = [];
        for(var i = 0; i < testArray.length; i++){
          var newTxt = testArray[i].label.toLowerCase();
            if(newTxt.indexOf(text) > -1){
                //console.log('found');
                newList.push(testArray[i]);
            }
        }
        if(newList.length > 0){
            loadList(newList)
```

```
                    return ;
            }
            //console.log('failed');
            return ;

        });

    });
    </script>
    </html>
```

In the preceding code, we actually instantiate a `datasource` object using the local array or data. These are all done when the page loads.

```
            datasource = new wijdatasource({
                reader: myReader,
                data: testArray,
                loaded: function (data){
                    // get items by data.items
                    loadList(data.items);
                }
            });
```

The `reader` property is set to `myReader`. This is the format for processing `testArray`, which is assigned to the `data` property of the `wijdatasource` object. The `loaded` function is called after the `wijdatasource` object is created, and it calls `loadList()`. This, in turn, renders the `wijlist` object in the `list` div. The functionality of the app, however, remains the same.

## There's more...

So far, we've demonstrated how to manipulate local data sources. The team at Wijmo was also aware of the possibilities of working with distributed systems that host data in remote locations, and thus provided a mechanism for digesting remote or distributed data sources over the network. This is achievable using the `proxy` property of the `wijdatasource` object. The proxy is set to the remote location of the data.

The following code was obtained from `http://wijmo.com/wiki/index.php/Datasource` and modified to function like our `wijdatasource` app, as was done previously, but makes use of a proxy now.

```
    <html>
    <head>
    <script src="http://ajax.aspnetcdn.com/ajax/jquery/jquery-1.7.1.min.
    js" type="text/javascript"></script>
    <script src="http://ajax.aspnetcdn.com/ajax/jquery.ui/1.8.17/jquery-
    ui.min.js" type="text/javascript"></script>
    <!--Wijmo Widgets JavaScript-->
```

```
<script src="http://cdn.wijmo.com/jquery.wijmo-open.all.2.0.0.min.js"
type="text/javascript"></script>
<script src="http://cdn.wijmo.com/jquery.wijmo-complete.all.2.0.0.min.
js" type="text/javascript"></script>
<!--Theme-->
<link href="http://cdn.wijmo.com/themes/rocket/jquery-wijmo.css"
rel="stylesheet" type="text/css" title="rocket-jqueryui" />
<!--Wijmo Widgets CSS-->
<link href="http://cdn.wijmo.com/jquery.wijmo-complete.all.2.0.0.min.
css" rel="stylesheet" type="text/css" />
<style>
input#testInput{width: 250px}
</style>
</head>
<body>
<div class="ui-widget">
    <P>Enter either whole or part of any of the following words
(representing some countries): "United States of America", "United
Arab Emirates", "Australia", "Canada", "Luxembourg", "Granada",
"Nigeria" or "Niger", then click the Load Data button. Data that
matches the whole or part of the value you entered, will be loaded
into the wijlist.</p>
    <input id="testInput" type="textbox" class="ui-widget-content ui-
corner-all" />
    <input type="button" id="loadData" value="Load Data" />
    <div id="list" style="height: 300px; width: 400px;"></div>
</div>
<script>
 $(document).ready(function () {
        $("#list").wijlist({});
        var proxy = new wijhttpproxy({
            url: "http://ws.geonames.org/searchJSON",
            dataType: "jsonp",
            data: {
                featureClass: "P",
                style: "full",
                maxRows: 10,
                name_startsWith: 'ab'
            },
            key: 'geonames'
        });
        var datasource = null;
        var thisData = null;
        var myReader = new wijarrayreader([
        {
```

```
                        name: 'label',
                        mapping: function (item){
                              return item.name + (item.adminName1 ? ", " + item.
      adminName1 : "") + ", " + item.countryName
                        }
                  },
                  {
                        name: 'value',mapping: 'name'
                  }
                  ]);
                        datasource = new wijdatasource({
                            reader: myReader,
                            proxy: proxy,
                            loaded: function (data){
                                  // get items by data.items
                                  thisData = data.items;
                                  loadList(data.items);


                              }
                  });
                  datasource.load();
                   function loadList(items){
                      var list = $("#list");
                      //set the array testArray to the Wijmo list widget
                      list.wijlist('setItems', items);
                      //Render the list in the client browser
                      list.wijlist('renderList');


                  }
                  $('#loadData').click(function(){

                      //process this section when the load Data is clicked...
                      var text = $('input#testInput').val().toLowerCase();
      proxy.options.data.name = text;
      datasource.load();
                      });

          });
      </script>
      </body>
      </html>
```

The preceding code pulls data from a proxy instead of local data. The data obtained has been limited to a maximum of 12, starting with `ab`. The functionality of our widget remains the same.

## See also

For more insight into `wijdatasources`, you can visit `http://wijmo.com/wiki/index.php/Datasource`. There are more configurations and options there that are very useful in customizing your widget.

# Using Wijmo with KnockoutJS (Advanced)

KnockoutJS is defined on their website `http://knockoutjs.com/documentation/introduction.html`, as follows:

> *Knockout is a JavaScript library that helps you to create rich, responsive display and editor user interfaces with a clean underlying data model.*

Any time you have sections of UI that update dynamically. Knockout can help you implement it more simply and is maintainable.

## Getting ready

Here is what Wijmo says about KnockoutJS:

Wijmo now supports Knockout (KO), a JavaScript library that uses the **Model View View Model** (**MVVM**) pattern, allowing you to easily create and maintain a dynamically changing UI. You can use KO in addition to jQuery to enhance your pages with an underlying data model. For a full KO introduction, tutorials, documentation, explanation of MVVM, and more, visit `http://knockoutjs.com/`.

Before we get started, note that this recipe is for anyone who has a prior familiarity with KnockoutJS, occasionally referred hereafter as KO. Please visit the KO website for an introduction if you are not familiar with it.

## How to do it...

You can easily use Knockout with Wijmo by following a few simple steps:

1. Add references to the latest jQuery dependencies, Wijmo widgets, `Knockout.js` file, and KO extension library for Wijmo.
2. Create the `ViewModel` and `View` objects: add JavaScript to define the data and behavior of the UI, and add markup to create `View`—the visual, interactive UI.
3. Bind the Wijmo widget(s) to `ViewModel` and activate KO.

Having known what both sides, Wijmo and Knockout, have to say about the awesome Knockout library, we can proceed by creating our first Knockout-integrated widget. First of all, to integrate the KnockoutJS library into our widgets, we would have to reference the Knockout files hosted in the Wijmo CDN as follows:

```
<script type="text/javascript" src="http://cdn.wijmo.com/external/
knockout-2.0.0.js"></script>
  <script type="text/javascript" src="http://cdn.wijmo.com/external/
knockout.wijmo.js"></script>
```

Assume we want to create an app or widget that can accept a measure of temperature in Celsius and return its Fahrenheit equivalent. For creating the input, we will have an input field that has a preset Celsius value and a linear gauge widget, also known as `wijlineargauge`, that will animate to the Fahrenheit-equivalent value. Enter the following code in your editor and run:

```
<!DOCTYPE html>
<html>
<head>
    <meta charset="utf-8">
    <title>Wijmo MVVM Support</title>
    <meta http-equiv="X-UA-Compatible" content="IE=edge,chrome=1" />
    <style type="text/css">
        body
        {
            font-size: 13px;
        }
    </style>
    <!-- jQuery -->
    <script type="text/javascript" src="https://ajax.googleapis.com/
ajax/libs/jquery/1.7.1/jquery.min.js"></script>
    <script type="text/javascript" src="https://ajax.googleapis.com/
ajax/libs/jqueryui/1.8.18/jquery-ui.min.js"></script>
    <!-- Wijmo CSS and script -->
    <link type="text/css" href="http://cdn.wijmo.com/themes/aristo/
jquery-wijmo.css" rel="stylesheet" title="metro-jqueryui" />
    <link type="text/css" href="http://cdn.wijmo.com/jquery.wijmo-
complete.all.2.1.0.min.css" rel="stylesheet" />
    <script type="text/javascript" src="http://cdn.wijmo.com/jquery.
wijmo-open.all.2.1.0.min.js"></script>
    <script type="text/javascript" src="http://cdn.wijmo.com/jquery.
wijmo-complete.all.2.1.0.min.js"></script>
    <!-- KnockoutJS for MVVM-->
    <script type="text/javascript" src="http://cdn.wijmo.com/external/
knockout-2.0.0.js"></script>
```

```html
    <script type="text/javascript" src="http://cdn.wijmo.com/external/
knockout.wijmo.js"></script>
    <script type="text/javascript">

    <!-- when document loads, create ViewModel, and apply bindings-->
    <!-- Create ViewModel-->

        var viewModel = function () {
            var self = this;
            self.celsius = ko.observable(20);
             self.kelvin = ko.computed(function(){
                //console.log('self.celsius = ' + self.celsius);
                return self.celsius() * 273;
            }, this);
            self.fahrenheit = ko.computed(function(){
                //console.log('self.celsius = ' + self.celsius);
                return self.celsius() * 1.8 + 32;
            }, this);
            self.min = ko.observable(0);
            self.max = ko.observable(200);
        };

    <!-- Bind ViewModel-->
        $(document).ready(function () {
            var vm = new viewModel();
            ko.applyBindings(vm);
        });
    </script>
</head>
<body>
    <div class="container">
        <h2>
            Celsius Textbox - Edit Here!</h2>
        <input data-bind="value: celsius" style="width: 200px;" />
        <div>
            <h2>
                Fahrenheit Slider - Don't Edit!</h2>
            <div data-bind="wijlineargauge: {value: fahrenheit, min:
min, max: max}" style="width: 800px;">
            </div>
        </div>
    </div>
</body>
</html>
```

## How it works...

If the code runs successfully, you should see the following image in your browser:

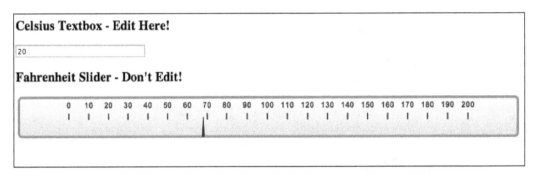

The Wijmo and Knockout libraries are referenced and included in our app. The `ViewModel` object is created, which has all the properties necessary for our app to function properly. The `self.celsius` property is an observable property, which is used to calculate `self.fahrenheit`. Also, `self.min` and `self.max` are used to set the minimum and maximum values of the gauge respectively. Then, we apply bindings of the `ViewModel` object to the view elements as shown in the following code:

```
ko.applyBindings(vm);
```

## There's more...

To finalize this recipe, we will create one more widget that will exhibit the beauty and overall importance of KO real-time data binding. This time we want to be able to update a simple pie chart right after a value entry for male and/or female.

Enter the following code in an editor and open it in a browser:

```
<!DOCTYPE html>
<html>
<head>
    <meta charset="utf-8">
    <title>Wijmo MVVM Support</title>
    <meta http-equiv="X-UA-Compatible" content="IE=edge,chrome=1" />
    <style type="text/css">
        body
        {
            font-size: 13px;
        }
    </style>
    <!-- jQuery -->
    <script type="text/javascript" src="https://ajax.googleapis.com/
ajax/libs/jquery/1.7.1/jquery.min.js"></script>
```

```
    <script type="text/javascript" src="https://ajax.googleapis.com/
ajax/libs/jqueryui/1.8.18/jquery-ui.min.js"></script>
    <!-- Wijmo CSS and script -->
    <link type="text/css" href="http://cdn.wijmo.com/themes/aristo/
jquery-wijmo.css" rel="stylesheet" title="metro-jqueryui" />
    <link type="text/css" href="http://cdn.wijmo.com/jquery.wijmo-
complete.all.2.1.0.min.css" rel="stylesheet" />
    <script type="text/javascript" src="http://cdn.wijmo.com/jquery.
wijmo-open.all.2.1.0.min.js"></script>
    <script type="text/javascript" src="http://cdn.wijmo.com/jquery.
wijmo-complete.all.2.1.0.min.js"></script>
    <!-- KnockoutJS for MVVM-->
    <script type="text/javascript" src="http://cdn.wijmo.com/external/
knockout-2.0.0.js"></script>
    <script type="text/javascript" src="http://cdn.wijmo.com/external/
knockout.wijmo.js"></script>
    <script type="text/javascript">

    <!-- when document loads, create ViewModel, and apply bindings-->
    <!-- Create ViewModel-->

        var viewModel = function () {
            var self = this;
            self.boys = ko.numericObservable(50);
            self.girls = ko.numericObservable(30);
        };

    <!-- Bind ViewModel-->
        $(document).ready(function () {
            var vm = new viewModel();
            ko.applyBindings(vm);
        });
    </script>
</head>
<body>
        <!--Create View-->
    <div>
        males: <input type="text" data-bind="value: boys" />
        females: <input type="text" data-bind="value: girls" />
    </div>
<div class="piechart" data-bind="wijpiechart: { width: 600, height:
400, seriesList:
                                                [{ label: 'Boys',
data: boys },
                                                { label:
'Girls', data: girls }
                                                ] }">
</div>
</body>
</html>
```

The preceding code sets up our `ViewModel` object with the boys and girls numeric observable properties. Our data is then bound to the views, and finally, we bind the `piechart` div to the `wijpiechart` object, passing the necessary values for the chart.

So far so good! This was easy, clean, and straightforward. One easily notices that the views and the view model are separate with only data bindings. In real-life software development, KO eliminates embedding server-side variables and dependencies within the views. The views should be purely HTML!

If successfully run, you will see a widget in your browser similar to the following screenshot:

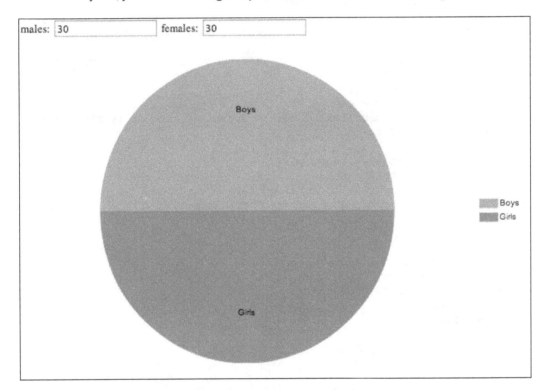

## ThemeRoller (Advanced)

Themes are an important part of any web or mobile widget. The quality, seamlessness, and ease of the user interface, also referred to as the UI, determine the usability of the widget. Most developers are less attentive to UI detail and focus more on the overall prototypical functionality.

The team at Wijmo understands the importance of UIs, and has integrated the jQuery UI into the Wijmo library. Wijmo was built on top of jQuery in such a way that making a reference to the Wijmo library also embeds the jQuery library.

## Getting ready

The essence of `ThemeRoller` is to enable us to customize the look and feel of our widgets or apps in general. All the sample widgets created in previous recipes have references to a Wijmo theme called `rocket`:

```
<link href="http://cdn.wijmo.com/themes/rocket/jquery-wijmo.css"
rel="stylesheet" type="text/css" title="rocket-jqueryui" />
```

This applies the `rocket` theme styles to the widget. So, to change the theme, we need to reference another one, preexisting or personally customized.

## How to do it...

1. To achieve this, we can make use of `jQuery ThemeRoller`, which is accessible at `http://jqueryui.com/themeroller/`.

2. Download a theme of your choice from the ones listed within the **Gallery** tab of the page. For the purposes of this tutorial, we are using **UI darkness**.

3. Click on the **Download** button below **UI darkness**; it takes you to the **Download Builder** page.

4. Now that we have downloaded the `jquery-ui-1.9.2.custom.zip` file, we need to unzip it. After extracting all the files, we navigate to the CSS file of our choice, minified or regular. For the purposes of this tutorial, we will use the minified version. There's not going to be much difference in performance, though.

5. The CSS file, in this case, is `jquery-ui-1.9.2.custom.min.css` and we have to include the path in our project, which will replace the rocket theme's CSS file as follows:

```
<link href=" jquery-ui-1.9.2.custom/css/ui-darkness/jquery-ui-
1.9.2.custom.min.css" rel="stylesheet" type="text/css" title="UI
darkness-jqueryui" />
```

6. We will redo one of the grid widgets using the new **UI darkness** theme we downloaded. Enter the following code in your editor and run it:

```html
<html>
<head>
<!--jQuery References-->
<script src="http://ajax.aspnetcdn.com/ajax/jquery/jquery-1.7.1.min.js" type="text/javascript"></script>
<script src="http://ajax.aspnetcdn.com/ajax/jquery.ui/1.8.17/jquery-ui.min.js" type="text/javascript"></script>
<!--Wijmo Widgets JavaScript-->
<script src="http://cdn.wijmo.com/jquery.wijmo-open.all.2.0.0.min.js" type="text/javascript"></script>
<script src="http://cdn.wijmo.com/jquery.wijmo-complete.all.2.0.0.min.js" type="text/javascript"></script>
<!--Theme-->
<link href="jquery-ui-1.9.2.custom/css/ui-darkness/jquery-ui-1.9.2.custom.min.css" rel="stylesheet" type="text/css" title="UI darkness-jqueryui" />
<!--Wijmo Widgets CSS-->
<link href="http://cdn.wijmo.com/jquery.wijmo-complete.all.2.0.0.min.css" rel="stylesheet" type="text/css" />
</head>
<body>
<table>
  <thead>
    <th>column0</th>
    <th>column1</th>
  </thead>
  <tbody>

  </tbody>
</table>

<script type="text/javascript">
var columns = [
    { headerText: 'First Name', dataKey: 'firstName', dataType: 'string'},
    { headerText: 'Last Name', dataKey: 'lastName', dataType: 'string' },
    { headerText: 'Date of Birth', dateKey: 'DOB', dataType: 'string' },
    { headerText: 'Occupation', dataKey: 'occupation', dataType: 'string' }
];
var content = [
    {
        firstName: 'Tochi',
```

```
                lastName: 'Eke-Okoro',
                DOB: '08/21',
                occupation: 'UI Developer'
        },
        {

                firstName: 'Ryan',
                lastName: 'Krest',
                DOB: '06/1',
                occupation: 'Attorney'
        },
        {

                firstName: 'Bruce',
                lastName: 'Romeo',
                DOB: '02/26',
                occupation: 'US Navy'
        }
    ];
    $("table").wijgrid({
        columns: columns,
        data: content
    });
    </script>
    </body>
    </html>
```

7.  If the preceding code is successfully run, you will see a Wijmo grid similar to this:

| First Name | Last Name | Date of Birth |
|---|---|---|
| Tochi | Eke-Okoro | 08/21 |
| Ryan | Krest | 06/1 |
| Bruce | Romeo | 02/26 |

Hurray! We have changed the theme for the widget!

## How it works...

The only thing we changed in our code was the reference or link to the theme or CSS file. We have used a theme we desire for our widget, and this is achievable as follows:

1.  Visit the **ThemeRoller** site at http://jqueryui.com/themeroller/.

2.  Click on the **Gallery** tab.

3.  In the **Gallery** section, you will find a list of themes. Click on the **Download** button below the theme of interest.

4. In the **Download Builder** page, turn on or off the options you do/don't need activated in your theme.

5. Overwrite the previous theme's path in your project with the new CSS file, which could be minified or regular.

6. There goes the new theme!

## There's more...

What about creating our own theme from scratch?

Its as easy as A-B-C!

The team at jQuery has provided a quick way of achieving this in ThemeRoller, which can be found at `http://jqueryui.com/themeroller/`. So, we'll visit the ThemeRoller site and we should be right on the **Roll Your Own** tab. You should be able to see this page:

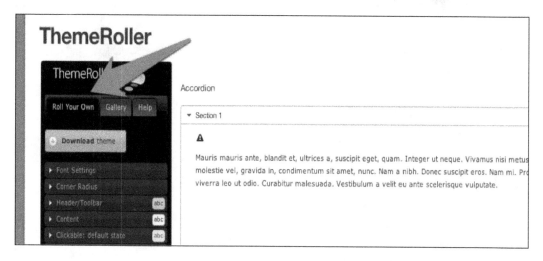

Open the **Header/Toolbar** and **Content** sections, and make some changes. The following screenshot shows the particular changes made for the purpose of this tutorial:

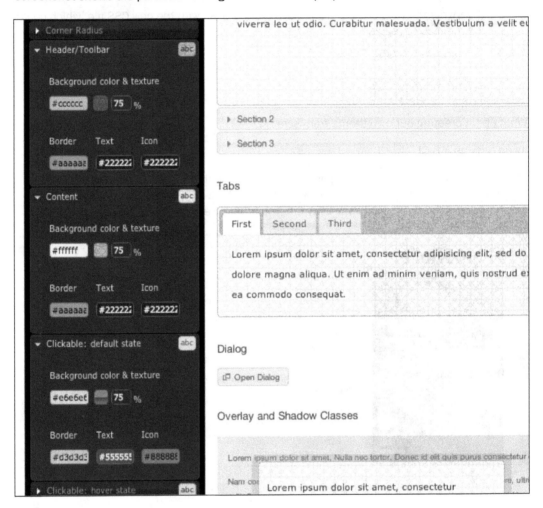

Next, click on the **Download Theme** button, which takes you to the **Download Builder** page. Here, you can turn the options on or off and then finally download the zipped theme. Unzip the file and add the path to your widget project. Navigate to the path and you will see the following screenshot:

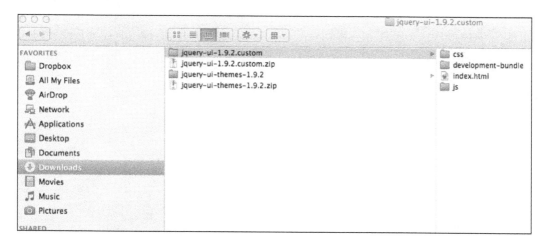

After switching from the theme reference and running the code, we have the following screen on our browser. This is the new look of our grid:

| First Name | Last Name | Date of Birth | |
|---|---|---|---|
| Tochi | Eke-Okoro | 08/21 | UI Deve |
| Ryan | Krest | 06/1 | Attorne |
| Bruce | Romeo | 02/26 | US Nav |

## See also

For more information on ThemeRollers, play around with the options and assets on the jQuery UI ThemeRoller site mentioned previously.

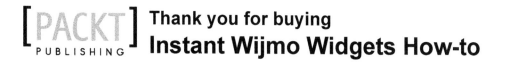

**Thank you for buying**
# Instant Wijmo Widgets How-to

## About Packt Publishing

Packt, pronounced 'packed', published its first book "*Mastering phpMyAdmin for Effective MySQL Management*" in April 2004 and subsequently continued to specialize in publishing highly focused books on specific technologies and solutions.

Our books and publications share the experiences of your fellow IT professionals in adapting and customizing today's systems, applications, and frameworks. Our solution based books give you the knowledge and power to customize the software and technologies you're using to get the job done. Packt books are more specific and less general than the IT books you have seen in the past. Our unique business model allows us to bring you more focused information, giving you more of what you need to know, and less of what you don't.

Packt is a modern, yet unique publishing company, which focuses on producing quality, cutting-edge books for communities of developers, administrators, and newbies alike. For more information, please visit our website: www.packtpub.com.

## Writing for Packt

We welcome all inquiries from people who are interested in authoring. Book proposals should be sent to author@packtpub.com. If your book idea is still at an early stage and you would like to discuss it first before writing a formal book proposal, contact us; one of our commissioning editors will get in touch with you.

We're not just looking for published authors; if you have strong technical skills but no writing experience, our experienced editors can help you develop a writing career, or simply get some additional reward for your expertise.

## Responsive Web Design with HTML5 and CSS3

ISBN: 978-1-84969-318-9          Paperback: 324 pages

Learn responsive design using HTML5 and CSS3 to adapt websites to any browser or screen size

1. Everything needed to code websites in HTML5 and CSS3 that are responsive to every device or screen size

2. Learn the main new features of HTML5 and use CSS3's stunning new capabilities including animations, transitions and transformations

3. Real world examples show how to progressively enhance a responsive design while providing fall backs for older browsers

## Learning jQuery

ISBN: 978-1-84719-250-9          Paperback: 380 pages

Better Interaction Design and Web Development with Simple JavaScript Techniques

1. Create better, cross-platform JavaScript code

2. Learn detailed solutions to specific client-side problems

3. For web designers who want to create interactive elements for their designs

4. For developers who want to create the best user interface for their web applications.

Please check **www.PacktPub.com** for information on our titles

## jQuery Tools UI Library

ISBN: 978-1-84951-780-5      Paperback: 112 pages

Learn jQuery Tools with clear, practical examples and get inspiration for developing your own ideas with the library

1. Learn how to use jQuery Tools, with clear, practical projects that you can use today in your websites

2. Learn how to use useful tools such as Overlay, Scrollable, Tabs and Tooltips

3. Full of practical examples and illustrations, with code that you can use in your own projects, straight from the book

## jQuery UI 1.8: The User Interface Library for jQuery

ISBN: 978-1-84951-652-5      Paperback: 424 pages

Build highly interactive web applications with ready-to-use widgets from the jQuery User Interface Library

1. Packed with examples and clear explanations of how to easily design elegant and powerful front-end interfaces for your web applications

2. A section covering the widget factory including an in-depth example on how to build a custom jQuery UI widget

3. Updated code with significant changes and fixes to the previous edition

Please check **www.PacktPub.com** for information on our titles

www.ingramcontent.com/pod-product-compliance
Lightning Source LLC
Chambersburg PA
CBHW060204060326
40690CB00018B/4241